WHO

POLICE PUBLIC CALL BOX

BBC Children's Books
Published by the Penguin Group
Penguin Books Ltd, 80 Strand, London, WC2R 0RL, England
Penguin Group (USA) Inc., 375 Hudson Street, New York, New York 10014, USA
Penguin Books (Australia) Ltd, 250 Camberwell Road, Camberwell, Victoria 3124, Australia.
(A division of Pearson Australia Group Pty Ltd)
Canada, India, New Zealand, South Africa
Published by BBC Children's Books, 2006
Text and design © Children's Character Books, 2006
Pages 6-11 and 23 written by Moray Laing
Pages 12-13, 25-29, 32-35, 38, 44-49 and 58 written by Davey Moore
Pages 15, 24, 36-37, 39, 41 and 56-57 written by Jacqueline Rayner
Pages 54-55 by Justin Richards
Pages 44-49 illustrations by John Ross
Pages 44-49 colours by James Offredi
Pages 16-21 originally published in Doctor Who Adventures. Written by Jacqueline Rayner, illustrated
by John Ross, coloured by Adrian Salmon.
10 9 8 7 6 5 4 3 2 1

ISBN-13: 978-1-40590-199-4
ISBN-10: 1-40590-199-3
Printed in Italy

All planet photography (except earth image) on pages 26, 27, 28 & 29 courtesy of NASA

WHO EXACTLY IS THE DOCTOR? DOCTOR WHO? WELL, THAT'S JUST IT. THE WHOLE OF TIME AND SPACE WOULDN'T BE THE SAME WITHOUT HIM AND NO ONE EVEN KNOWS HIS WHOLE NAME. SO, WHAT DO WE KNOW?

The Doctor may look, talk and dress like a human, but he is actually an alien with two hearts He is also a long, long way from home. His planet was destroyed in the Time War along with all his people, the Time Lords, making the Doctor the only survivor of a once powerful race.

Travelling through time and space in his amazing TARDIS, which stands for Time And Relative Dimension In Space, he usually knows what to do when times get rough. He's a lone Time Lord with a fierce sense of what's right and what's wrong. And if you were to meet him, you'd want to be his friend. Here is a man you could trust with your life.

He also happens to be over 900 years old with the ability to change his body when it becomes old or damaged. This handy process, called regeneration, is a Time Lord's way of cheating death. And isn't very predictable as Rose Tyler found out when the Doctor absorbed all the energy of the Time Vortex.

To everyone but the Doctor, swallowing the Time Vortex would have been deadly. It would have killed Rose if the Doctor hadn't rescued her. When the regeneration process kicked in, the Doctor exploded in a blast of energy and changed his appearance. As Rose watched in horror and confusion, the man who she had shared so many dangerous adventures with simply disappeared... and in his place, stood a smiling younger man. A new Doctor. Same man, new face, ready for new adventures!

And long before the Doctor met Rose, he had regenerated several times already...

THE BEGINNING

Long ago, the original Doctor appeared to be a much older man. With white hair and a quick temper, he wasn't the sort of person you would want to get on the wrong side of. He was also quick to bark at those who angered him. Hard to believe this older figure is the same Doctor we know today.

Two teachers were having problems with a girl at their school and decided to follow the girl home and confront her grandfather, a 'Doctor' who apparently didn't like strangers. Her home turned out to be a police box that was an incredible space and time machine that was bigger on the inside than out. The Doctor was convinced that the teachers would tell everybody about his ship so he kidnapped them...

And so it began — adventures in time and space with two teachers and a mysterious old man and young girl from another planet. They didn't talk much of their home world, but one thing was for sure — they were never going to go back.

The Doctor didn't have much control over his time machine. He never knew if the TARDIS would end up in the future or the past, let alone the present. If working properly it should have been able to appear at any precise moment in time and space and also be able to change its appearance to blend in with its surroundings. The old ship was slightly damaged and became stuck in the distinctive shape of a blue Earth police box.

During these adventures, many, like Rose, Captain Jack and Mickey, would step aboard the TARDIS and travel for a time before settling down. Some got home. Some didn't. Some even stayed in completely different times to those they were born in.

ALL CHANGE

And then one day, without much warning, the Doctor complained that his body was getting old and wearing a bit thin. He collapsed, his features blurred and he changed...

It's understandable that his companions at the time, like Rose, couldn't quite understand what had happened to the Doctor. Well, face it, would you trust your best friend if they changed their face one day without telling you they could?

Over the years the Doctor has changed appearance several times. He's looked older. He's looked younger. He's been louder and brasher. But always wise and always the same Doctor at heart. Or hearts.

THE CONSTANT TRAVELLER

So why doesn't he settle down? Why does he never stay still? Is it because "trouble is just the bits in between", as he once told Rose's mum? After all, it's a big universe out there and with all of time to explore too, there are endless places to visit.

He's a traveller with a thirst for knowledge and he'll stop at nothing to help others when he can. But, as he's found out, he can't always help everyone. Even his best friend Rose...

He's saved the Earth more times than we possibly realise — everything from the Wire and the Gelth to the Daleks and the Cybermen... but at what cost? One thing's for sure, while the Doctor and the TARDIS travel through time and space, the universe is a safer place.

IT'S NOT EVERYONE WHO GETS THE CHANCE TO TRAVEL IN THE TARDIS. THE DOCTOR ONLY TAKES THE BEST...

ROSE

Rose Tyler. The Doctor's best friend. When she got out of bed one morning to go to her boring job in a department store, nothing could have prepared her for the exciting times ahead. On that day, shop dummies came to life and tried to kill her, but luckily she was rescued by the Doctor. Later, when the Doctor asked her if she wanted to travel with him in his TARDIS she said no. She couldn't possibly leave her life behind and jump inside an alien spaceship with a stranger and go travelling. She had Mickey to look after, and then there was her mum to think about...

Or could she? Things would be so different if she'd gone home, but when the Doctor explained that he could also travel through time, Rose ran through those doors... into the time of her life.

And what a life! She's seen the end of the world, prevented World War Three, and met her Dad twice, a man who she had never known. Strong and brave and not someone to give up easily, she has saved the Earth from Daleks and Cybermen, and rescued the Doctor from all sorts of trouble including the Nestene Conscience and Isolus. The Doctor without Rose is difficult to imagine...

SARAH JANE SMITH

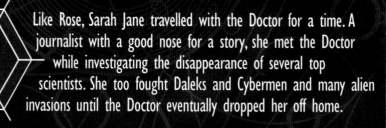

Like Rose, Sarah Jane travelled with the Doctor for a time. A journalist with a good nose for a story, she met the Doctor while investigating the disappearance of several top scientists. She too fought Daleks and Cybermen and many alien invasions until the Doctor eventually dropped her off home.

Or so he thought. Unfortunately for Sarah Jane, the Doctor got it wrong. Instead of Croydon as promised, the TARDIS left her miles away in Aberdeen without realising! The Doctor didn't find this out until the old friends bumped into each other many years later.

Sarah Jane and Rose didn't exactly hit it off immediately when they were introduced to each other, but by the end of their dangerous encounter with the Krillitanes, realised they had much in common. They both needed the Doctor in their life — it was a better place with him there — and they loved their life with him. When the Doctor suggested Sarah Jane joins them on their travels she must have been tempted. But no, she chose to stay and get on with her life on Earth. A life she shares with another old friend of the Doctor's — K-9.

K-9

With a fantastic computer brain, K-9 is much more than just a robot. Like a loyal pet, he faithfully protects his friends from danger at all times, with the ability to stun or blast enemies.

There have been several versions of the robot dog, K-9. The original was given to the Doctor in the year 5000AD. The Doctor built a further two models, one of which he left with Sarah Jane on Earth. This version lived with her until he broke down and, because the alien technology was difficult to repair, Sarah Jane left him rusting like an abandoned toy.

The Doctor repaired this model, but only just. With failing batteries, K-9 gave up his life in order to destroy the Krillitanes. Sarah Jane was clearly very upset and the Doctor left her a new K-9 with improved systems to look after her.

REINETTE

The beautiful Reinette Poisson, also known as Madame de Pompadour, knew the Doctor all her life. When confused repair droids thought that a 37-year-old Reinette was the key to repairing their damaged ship, they opened up time windows in an attempt to track her down...

As the Doctor jumped between different times he met Reinette as a girl, a young lady, and eventually a woman as he tried to protect her from the dangerous clockwork droids.

Reinette, although at first confused by the man who would appear from her fireplace, always looked forward to her meetings with the Doctor. He was the only man she ever loved and they seemed to understand each other.

And Reinette meant a lot to the Doctor, too. He was prepared to become trapped in the past with her. When they discovered that a link was still open to the spaceship, he was ready to take her back to the TARDIS to travel with him, Rose and Mickey, an offer that excited her greatly. But, tragically, when the Doctor returned to collect Reinette, years had passed, and she was already dead.

To car mechanic Mickey, the Doctor meant danger and aliens, and at first he found it difficult to see what Rose found so exciting about travelling around the universe in an old police box. He watched as Rose ran from him into the TARDIS and off to unknown danger, and to begin with, he didn't think much of the Doctor.

While Rose was witnessing the end of the world and meeting Charles Dickens, a year passed. Poor Mickey was left to get on with living alone until Rose walked back into his life as if she had only been away a few days...

When he helped prevent World War Three, the Doctor asked him if he'd like to join Rose and him on their travels, but Mickey wasn't ready. It wasn't until he'd helped defeat the Krillitanes and met Sarah Jane that he was ready to travel in the TARDIS.

But after travelling to a parallel Earth, helping defeat the Cybermen, and even meeting his parallel self, Mickey realised he'd always be in the shadow of the Doctor so chose to stay on the different Earth. Mickey thought he would never see Rose, or the Doctor, again...

Jackie loves her daughter Rose more than anything in the world. So when the Doctor walked into their life and took her away, the Doctor was not at the top of her list of favourite people. It took some time before she trusted him. It wasn't until he sent Rose back to her, while he attempted to stop a future Dalek invasion of Earth, that Jackie realized the Doctor was a man of his word, and he would protect her daughter at all costs.

Not afraid of saying what she means and with a tendency to flare up when she's angry, Jackie has seen shop dummies come to life, the Slitheen take over London, the dramatic Sycorax invasion, and of course, the battle between the Cybermen and the Daleks.

Over time, she's given the Doctor a second chance and even helped to save his life. She's always known that Rose is following her heart and doing exactly what she wants to do. Perhaps if Jackie had been given the chance she would have wanted to go travelling in time and space too...

PETE TYLER

Rose's father, Pete, died before Rose was old enough to remember him, so she grew up only knowing what Jackie would tell her. Unknown to her, Jackie and Pete hadn't always got on and they annoyed each other for most of their marriage. He was always having get-rich-quick ideas... such as selling health drinks like Vitex. None of which came to anything. Not in our world, anyway.

It took a few trips in the TARDIS before Rose decided to ask the Doctor if they could go back and visit her dad, before he died. Meet the dad she never knew. When they did, she prevented him from being run down by a car and in doing so caused a rift in time and released the horrific Reapers.

Pete worked out that the only way to save his daughter, and the world, from the Reapers was to throw himself in front of the car that was originally meant to kill him. During the precious extra hours of his life, Pete gets the chance to see his grown-up daughter and is extremely proud of her. He died while Rose watched.

In the parallel world that the Doctor, Rose and Mickey visit, Pete Tyler has become a successful businessman working for Cybus Industries. But Pete is also a mole, passing information about Cybus Industries to the Preachers, via an encrypted radio station, to help them defeat the Cybermen.

HARRIET JONES

Harriet Jones was MP for Flydale North, when she met the Doctor and Rose. She was one of the first people to discover the Slitheen had invaded 10 Downing Street and were killing members of the Cabinet. Alongside the time travellers, she helped prevent World War III and hid with them inside the Cabinet Room while a bomb struck the building and destroyed the Slitheen.

When the Doctor met Harriet Jones for the second time, she had become Prime Minister and the Earth was at the mercy of the Sycorax invasion. Knowing that someone like the Doctor was the Earth's only hope, she even put out a plea for his help on television.

As the Sycorax left Earth in their mighty spaceship, she controversially gave the order to the Torchwood Institute to destroy it. The Doctor was appalled at her decision, and walked away from Harriet, saddened at her decision to destroy aliens who had agreed to leave in peace.

IT'S A VAST UNIVERSE AND IT CAN BE LONELY OUT THERE, SO IT'S A GOOD JOB THE DOCTOR HAS HAD MANY COMPANIONS ON HIS JOURNEY THROUGH TIME AND SPACE. FOLLOW THIS FLOWCHART AND FIND OUT WHICH OF THE DOCTOR'S COMPANIONS YOU'RE MOST LIKE.

START
Would you enjoy an adventure holiday?
YES / NO

Is your family important to you?
YES / NO

Do you enjoy taking risks?
NO / YES

Do you prefer computer games to team games?
YES / NO

START
Do you look towards the future, or think about the past?
FUTURE / PAST

Do you prefer to study Science, or Art?
SCIENCE / ART

Do you like to travel, or stay at home?
STAY HOME / TRAVEL

Is your best friend a little bit crazy?
YES / NO

Would you say that you're your own best friend?
YES / NO

Do you sometimes feel like the odd one out?
NO / YES

Are you the life and soul of a party?
YES / NO

START
Do you like to take things apart to see how they work?
YES / NO

Do you find other people confusing?
YES / NO

Do you love discovering new things?
YES / NO

FIND

If you lose something, do you forget about it, or try to find it?
FIND / FORGET

Are you good at cracking codes?
YES / NO

START
Are you always up for a new challenge?
YES / NO

Uh-oh. Here comes a Dalek. Do you attempt to talk to it?
NO / YES

Do you feel ready to settle in one place?
YES

Have you ever met someone who looks exactly like you?

YES →

NO ↓

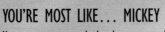

YOU'RE MOST LIKE... MICKEY

You are an extremely loyal person, and sometimes that loyalty leads you into trouble or adventures you never suspected you might have. You're basically a nice guy, but didn't anyone tell you that nice guys finish last? Try to toughen up, if you do, you might just end up saving the day!

Are looks important to you?

NO →

YES ↓

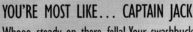

YOU'RE MOST LIKE... ROSE

You have a big heart and, no matter how dark things get, you always look on the bright side. Your sunny disposition brings out the best in the people around you. But, be careful! Sometimes, just like a cat, your curiosity can get you into trouble!

Would you give up everything for someone you'd just met?

YES →

NO ↓

YOU'RE MOST LIKE... CAPTAIN JACK

Whooo, steady on there, fella! Your swashbuckling, devil-may-care attitude only works if you're handsome and charming too! So check yourself out in the mirror before you go wading in. Sometimes you're a little bit selfish. Keep in mind that it helps to open up to others and always remember your friends.

Are you good at fixing things?

YES →

NO ↓

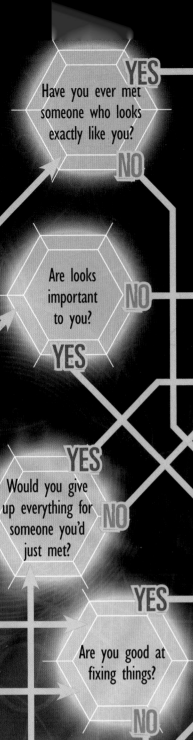

YOU'RE MOST LIKE... K-9

It's amazing that you've bothered to follow this flow chart to its logical conclusion as, frankly, you are a bit of a funsucker! There are advantages to having an analytical mind and a tell-it-like-it-is personality, but you might think about choosing a job in science rather than politics.

Have you ever answered a question with the words "Insufficient data"?

YES →

NO ↓

Do you believe a dog is a man's best friend?

YES →

YOU'RE MOST LIKE...SARAH JANE

You've had your share of adventures in your time, but there has come a point where you'd prefer a quiet life! Don't forget how much fun you had though, and if the opportunity for a new adventure arises, think carefully before you make your decision...

CASSANDRA

WITH A TEXAN FATHER AND A MOTHER FROM THE ARCTIC DESERT, LADY CASSANDRA O'BRIEN DOT DELTA SEVENTEEN CONSIDERS HERSELF TO BE THE LAST PURE HUMAN. WHEN THE DOCTOR AND ROSE FIRST MEET HER ON PLATFORM ONE, AT THE END OF THE WORLD PARTY, SHE IS ALREADY OVER 2,000 YEARS OLD AND HAS HAD OVER 708 OPERATIONS.

6ft tall, 3ft wide but only 1 inch deep

Wrinkles cut out by surgeons

Eyes salvaged from bin on Platform One

Skin taken from the back of the human Cassandra's body, and strapped to a metal frame

Can see straight through her when she talks

Cassandra created a psychograft, which allowed her brain to enter other people's bodies.

Cassandra built a force-grown-clone called Chip, to look after her.

Before all her operations, Cassandra really was very beautiful.

Cassandra's brain survived after her old skin snapped on Platform One

MONSTER HUNT

15

FILL IN THE ANSWERS AND THE YELLOW SQUARES WILL REVEAL A MONSTER!

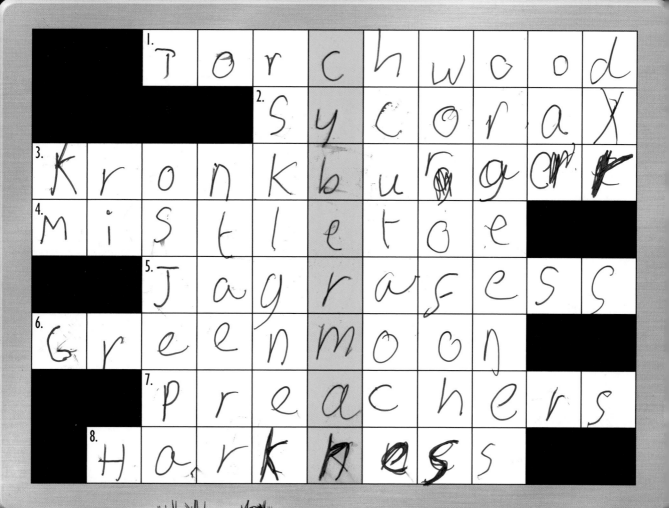

1. Torchwood
2. Sycorax
3. Kronkburger
4. Mistletoe
5. Jagrafess
6. Greenmoon
7. preachers
8. Harkness

1. Sir Robert MacLeish's house.
2. Aliens who invaded at Christmas.
3. Fast food available on Satellite Five.
4. Parasitic plant hated by werewolves.
5. Evil alien behind Satellite Five.
6. Universal symbol for hospitals.
7. Rebel organisation run by Ricky.
8. Captain Jack's surname.

THE KRILLITANES ARE COMPOSITE ALIENS, MADE UP OF ALL THE DIFFERENT RACES THEY HAVE CONQUERED. THEY HAVE CREATED THEMSELVES FROM ALL THE BEST PHYSICAL ATTRIBUTES OF OTHER ALIENS. THE LAST TIME THE DOCTOR CAME ACROSS THEM, THEY LOOKED LIKE HUMANS WITH REALLY LONG NECKS!

KRILLITANES

Bat-like wings stolen from a race in Bessan

Human form is a simple morphic illusion, with the true Krillitanes form hidden underneath.

Super-sensitive hearing

Compulsory school dinners contain Krillitane oil, which improved the children's concentration and performance.

Nightmarish shriek calls the other Krillitanes

Diet consists primarily of human children and other living creatures

The Krillitanes used the children's imaginations to try and crack the Skasas Paradigm, which would give them control of the universe.

IF THE KRILLITANES HAD TAKEN OVER YOUR SCHOOL, WOULD YOU HAVE NOTICED? FOLLOW THIS GUIDE TO MAKE SURE YOU AND YOUR FRIENDS ARE PREPARED FOR ALIEN INVASION. THE SIGNS ARE ALWAYS THERE. YOU'VE JUST GOT TO KNOW WHAT TO LOOK FOR.

1 GAS EXCHANGE

Does your teacher fart a lot? Be careful! This telltale sign means that your teacher could be part of the missing Slitheen family from Raxacoricofallapatorious. A Slitheen could be inside your favourite teacher's body...the farting comes from the gas exchange, which enables the alien to fit inside a human body.

2 PSYCHIC

Does your teacher know when you are about to do something bad? If you are planning a trick, like pretending to be ill so you can go home early, don't! If you have tried this and your teacher has accused you of making it up, they could have special alien psychic powers.

3 LANGUAGE

Do you sometimes not understand what they are saying? Perhaps the translation unit in their voice box is faulty, resulting in alien babble. This is a sure sign they are from another planet.

4 EYES

Look very closely. Do your teacher's eyes glow? Suggest your teacher goes into a dark cupboard and watch to see if their eyes turn green or red to adjust to the light. If yes, close the cupboard door and run...

5 ENVIRONMENT

Do you only ever see them at school? Perhaps their spaceship is buried under the playground and they have no proper home to return to. Watch where they go when school is over for the day.

6 CLOTHES

What are they wearing? Do they wear lots of corduroy? Many aliens who pose as teachers think a pair of cords is an acceptable 'teacher' look. Like the Krillitanes, however, they might look a bit too perfect. Too clean. Too immaculate. It can be quite tricky to spot the aliens sometimes!

7 SMELL

If you dare to get close enough, check out the breath of your teacher. Is it rancid and like a particularly smelly dog's? If yes, your teacher could be from the outer reaches of the galaxy, where personal hygiene has never been too important.

8 MEALS

Carefully monitor their eating habits. Have you seen what and how they eat at lunchtime? If not, try to observe. Aliens find it difficult eating with their mouths closed and with cutlery.

9 NAILS

Look at their fingernails. Never trust anyone with long dirty ones. Most aliens fail to keep their nails trim and clean, so this can be an obvious sign.

10 STARE

Many aliens don't blink as much as humans. In your next lesson, count the number of times your teacher blinks. If it is less than three times, they might not be human...

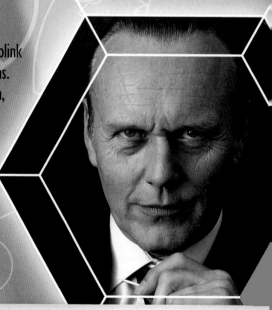

MEMORISE THESE SIGNS IMMEDIATELY! AND IF YOU THINK YOUR TEACHER MIGHT BE AN ALIEN, REPORT THEM TO THE HEAD TEACHER NOW. UNLESS, OF COURSE, YOUR HEAD TEACHER FARTS A LOT, HAS BAD BREATH, AND YOU'VE NEVER SEEN THEM BLINKING... TAKE CARE!

FOLLOWING THE SUCCESSFUL DEFEAT OF THE KRILLITANES, THE DOCTOR-MASTER, MISTRESS SARAH JANE, ROSE, MICKEY AND KENNY PLANNED TO CELEBRATE WITH THE CONSUMPTION OF BEVERAGES.

However, while they were awaiting the arrival of refreshment, a localized ion storm caused a temporary disturbance in the particles of the brains of all living organisms in the vicinity.

When the human waiter arrived with the tray of beverages: tea, coffee, ginger beer, cola and orange juice, those present were unable to recall who had initiated the purchase of each individual liquid. Or as the Doctor-Master put it, "We've all forgotten who ordered what."

My own superior electronic cells were only mildly affected, and therefore I was able to retrieve data from my memory banks pertaining to the beverage ownership controversy. However, with the confusion from the ion storm ongoing, we are unable to focus our logic circuits on the current problem. Can you help?

I have manufactured a table to facilitate the logical application, and have succeeded in translating the first clue to assist in the conclusion.

DATA

FACT 1: Mistress Sarah does not like ginger beer.

FACT 2: Rose and Mickey's drinks begin with the same letter.

FACT 3: Either the Doctor-Master or Mistress Sarah Jane has a hot drink, but not both.

FACT 4: Kenny is not allowed fizzy drinks.

FACT 5: Mickey did not order a cold drink.

	TEA	COFFEE	GINGER BEER	COLA	ORANGE JUICE
DOCTOR					
ROSE					
MICKEY					
SARAH JANE			X		
KENNY					

THE DOCTOR ORDERED _____   SARAH JANE ORDERED _____

ROSE ORDERED _____   KENNY ORDERED _____

MICKEY ORDERED _____

DOCTOR HO HO!

IT'S A TOUGH JOB BEING THE LAST TIME LORD, BUT EVEN THE DOCTOR HAS TO HAVE A LAUGH FROM TIME TO TIME. HERE'S A CLUSTER OF JOKES TO KEEP HIM — AND YOU — CHUCKLING THROUGH HYPERSPACE.

HOW CAN YOU TELL A SLITHEEN IS AN ALIEN?
Because it's only got one 'i'!

WHERE DOES A CYBERMAN LEAVE HIS SPACESHIP?
At a parking meteor!

WHERE DO DALEKS GO TO BUY CHEESE?
To a Dalek-atessen!

WHAT TIME IS IT WHEN A DALEK RUNS OVER YOUR FOOT?
Time to call the Doctor!

FIRST CYBERMAN: I'm hungry.
SECOND CYBERMAN: So am I, it must be launch time!

WHAT DO YOU GET IF YOU CROSS THE MIGHTY JAGRAFESS OF THE HOLY HADROJASSIC MAXARODENFOE WITH PEANUT BUTTER?
A monster that sticks to the roof of your mouth.

WHY DID THE FACE OF BOE GO TO A PARTY ON HIS OWN?
Because he didn't have any body to go with.

DID YOU HEAR ABOUT THE SLITHEEN BEAUTY CONTEST?
Nobody won.

WHAT DO YOU GET IF YOU CROSS A DALEK WITH A DOG?
Very nervous postmen!

HOW DO YOU GET THE MIGHTY JAGRAFESS INTO A MATCHBOX?
Take all the matches out first.

WHAT'S THE BEST WAY TO NEGOTIATE WITH A CYBERMAN?
From a long way away!

CAN A DALEK JUMP HIGHER THAN A LAMP POST?
Yes — lamp posts can't jump.

WHAT IS THE BEST WAY TO SEE A CYBERMAN?
On television!

IF STORKS BRING HUMAN BABIES, WHAT BRINGS DALEK BABIES?
Cranes.

WHAT BOUNCES UP AND DOWN SAYING "EXTERMINATE!"?
A Dalek on a pogo stick.

DID YOU HEAR ABOUT THE TIME TRAVELLING COW?
Its name was Doctor Moo.

WHY DIDN'T THE DOCTOR LIKE IT WHEN ROSE BROUGHT HER BOYFRIEND INTO THE TARDIS?
He thought she was taking the Mickey!

WHY DID MICKEY WANT TO TRAVEL INTO SPACE?
Because he was no earthly good!

WHAT DID ROSE TYLER HAVE FOR TEA?
An unidentified frying object.

TO TRAVEL THROUGH SPACE LIKE THE DOCTOR, IT REALLY HELPS TO KNOW A BIT ABOUT IT! THE SOLAR SYSTEM IS THE GROUP OF PLANETS, AND THEIR MOONS, WHICH ORBIT THE STAR KNOWN AS THE SUN. THERE ARE NINE KNOWN PLANETS, INCLUDING EARTH, IN OUR SOLAR SYSTEM — LET'S FIND OUT ABOUT THEM!

MERCURY

Mercury is a dense, fast moving planet with a large iron core and a thin crust of silicate rock. It rotates on its axis slower than it orbits the sun, so its day is longer than its year!

AVERAGE DISTANCE FROM SUN: 57.9 million km

EQUATORIAL DIAMETER: 4,880 km

Being so close to the sun, and having an atmosphere so thin it barely exists, Mercury's surface temperature can soar to an extremely hot 450°C during the day while plummeting to as low as -180°C at night!

VENUS

Venus is a similar size to Earth and is our nearest planetary neighbour. It spins slowly on its axis in the opposite direction to most other planets.

AVERAGE DISTANCE FROM SUN: 108.2 million km

DIAMETER: 12,104 km

Venus can be seen from Earth by the naked eye. It shines brightly in our sky and is named after the Roman goddess of love and beauty.

EARTH

Earth is the only planet in the Solar System with liquid water on its surface, and an atmosphere rich in oxygen.

AVERAGE DISTANCE FROM SUN: 149.6 million km

EQUATORIAL DIAMETER: 12,756 km

In ancient times, it was believed the Earth, not the Sun, was the centre of the Solar System.

THE MOON

BONUS CARD!

While the planets orbit around the Sun, many of the planets have moons that orbit around them. Earth has one moon.

AVERAGE DISTANCE FROM EARTH: 384,400 km

EQUATORIAL DIAMETER: 3,476 km

Our calendar months are based on the amount of time it takes the moon to go through its phases — 29.53 days.

MARS

Mars was named after the Roman god of war because of its blood red colour. The planet's red appearance is due to high quantities of iron oxide in the soil.

AVERAGE DISTANCE FROM SUN: 227.9 million km

EQUATORIAL DIAMETER: 6,794 km

The surface of Mars is an amazing sight, its volcanoes and canyons are much bigger than those found on Earth.

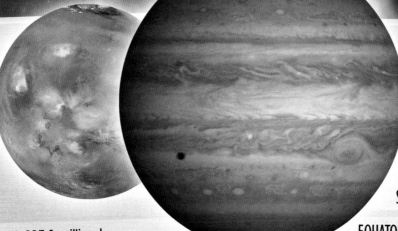

JUPITER

Jupiter is the giant of the Solar System — it is eleven times wider than Earth!

AVERAGE DISTANCE FROM SUN: 778.4 million km

EQUATORIAL DIAMETER: 142,984 km

Jupiter was once five times the size it is now! It shrinks by about 2cm every year.

SATURN

Saturn is nine times wider than the Earth. It is a large ball of liquid and gas topped by clouds.

AVERAGE DISTANCE FROM SUN: 1.427 billion km

EQUATORIAL DIAMETER: 120,536 km

Saturn has eighteen moons but it is most recognizable for its rings, which are composed of particles of dust and ice.

URANUS

Earth's axis is tipped 23.5º, whereas Uranus tilts from the vertical by 98º! Uranus has extremely long seasons, as each pole has 42 years of continuous sunlight, followed by 42 years of darkness.

AVERAGE DISTANCE FROM SUN: 2.871 billion km

EQUATORIAL DIAMETER: 51,118 km

Uranus' 17 moons were named after characters from the writings of Alexander Pope and William Shakespeare.

NEPTUNE

Neptune's largest moon is called Triton. It is bigger than the planet Pluto, and orbits in the opposite direction to Neptune's seven other moons!

AVERAGE DISTANCE FROM SUN: 4.498 billion km

EQUATORIAL DIAMETER: 49,532 km

Neptune is 30 times farther from the Sun than Earth.

PLUTO

Pluto is the smallest planet (even smaller than Earth's moon) and the farthest from the sun. It takes Pluto 247.68 Earth years to orbit the Sun.

AVERAGE DISTANCE FROM SUN: 5.9 billion km

EQUATORIAL DIAMETER: 2,274 km

The sun appears a thousand times fainter from Pluto, than it does from Earth.

SO YOU KNOW ALL ABOUT THE ADVENTURES OF DOCTOR WHO — BUT HOW MUCH DO YOU KNOW ABOUT YOUR OWN SOLAR SYSTEM? (IF YOU'VE LOOKED AT THE PREVIOUS PAGES THEN, HOPEFULLY, THE ANSWER IS, "QUITE A BIT!") HAVE A GO AT THIS QUIZ AND SEE IF YOU'RE MORE CLUED-UP THAN CAPTAIN JACK, AND LESS SPACED OUT THAN MICKEY!

THE SOLAR SYSTEM

There are nine planets in our Solar System.
What do you know about them?

1. WHICH PLANET IS THE CLOSEST TO THE EARTH?

2. WHICH PLANET HAS A LONGER 'DAY' THAN 'YEAR'?

3. THE LARGEST PLANET IS ALSO THE FASTEST SPINNING — BUT WHICH IS IT?

4. WHICH PLANET IS TIPPED SO FAR OVER THAT IT APPEARS TO LIE ON ITS SIDE?

5. THE OLYMPUS MONS IS THE HIGHEST MOUNTAIN IN THE SOLAR SYSTEM. WHICH PLANET IS IT ON?

6. WHICH PLANET IS SMALLER THAN EARTH'S MOON?

7. JULIET, CRESSIDA AND DESDEMONA ARE MOONS OF WHICH PLANET?

8. WHICH PLANET'S TEMPERATURE VARIES WILDLY FROM DAY TO NIGHT?

9. NAME ONE OF THE TWO PLANETS THAT ROTATE THE OPPOSITE WAY TO ALL THE OTHERS.

10. WHICH OF THESE STATEMENTS IS NOT TRUE?
A) Mercury has the greatest variation in night and day temperatures.
B) Mars has bigger volcanoes and canyons than Earth.
C) Neptune's largest moon is Triton.
D) Saturn's rings are made of particles of ice and dust.
E) Pluto is the biggest planet in the solar system.

THE MOON

The Moon is about one-quarter the size of Earth and we see it almost every night — but how much do you know about it?

11. IN WHAT YEAR DID A PERSON FIRST SET FOOT ON THE MOON?
A) 2001.
B) 1995.
C) 1306.
D) 1969.

12. WHAT WAS THE NAME OF THE FIRST SUCCESSFUL MISSION TO THE MOON?
A) Bad Wolf.
B) Apollo.
C) Operation Moon.
D) Lunar Explorer.

13. WHAT IS RESPONSIBLE FOR MOST OF THE CRATERS ON THE MOON'S SURFACE?
A) Alien caves.
B) Volcanoes.
C) Meteorites.
D) Spaceships.

14. THE ALPS IS A MOUNTAIN RANGE ON THE MOON — TRUE OR FALSE?

15. WHICH OF THESE THINGS HAS THE MOON BEEN THOUGHT RESPONSIBLE FOR?
A) The tides of the sea.
B) Turning people into werewolves.
C) Giving power to witches.
D) Influencing our calendar.

EARTH

Earth is the only planet we know of that has any liquid water on its surface. There must have been running water on Mars at some point (dried up river beds show this) but not any more.

16. WHAT PERCENTAGE OF THE EARTH'S SURFACE IS COVERED BY WATER?
A) 100%.
B) 5%.
C) 50%.
D) 71%.

17. WHICH OF THESE MAN-MADE OBJECTS CAN BE SEEN FROM SPACE?
A) The Great Wall of China.
B) Hadrian's Wall.
C) The Torchwood Institute.
D) The Empire State Building.

18. WHO PUBLISHED HIS LAWS OF GRAVITY IN 1687?
A) William Shakespeare.
B) John Lumic.
C) Sir Isaac Newton.
D) Alexander Pope.

19. THE EARTH IS PERFECTLY SPHERICAL — TRUE OF FALSE?

And a really tricky one to finish off;

20. WHAT IS THE NAME OF THE SCIENCE THAT DEALS WITH THE SIZE AND SHAPE OF THE EARTH?

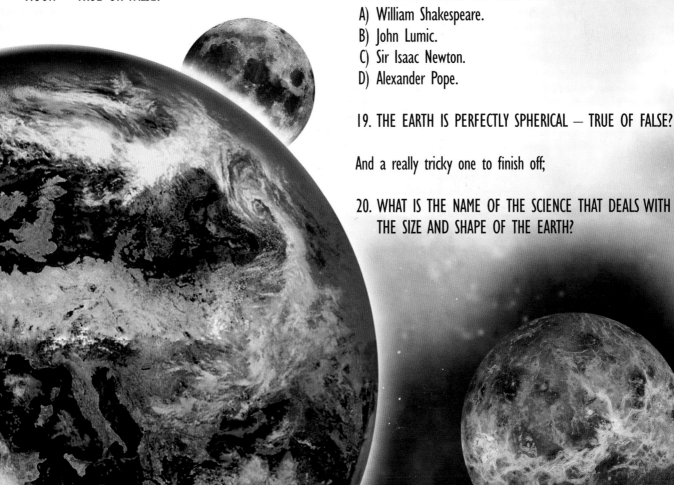

OOD

THE OOD COME FROM FAR AWAY IN THE HORSEHEAD NEBULA. THEY USED TO BE CONTROLLED BY A HIVE MIND, WHICH WAS DESTROYED BY HUMAN COLONISTS. THE DISCONNECTED OOD THEN BECAME A SLAVE RACE, AND LIVED TO SERVE MANKIND. THEY ONLY BECAME AN ENEMY WHEN THEIR MINDS WERE CONTROLLED BY THE BEAST...

A low-level telepathic field connects all the Ood and allows them to communicate internally with each other and receive telepathic orders

Eyes glow red when the Ood are being controlled by the Beast

Hand-balls allow them to communicate with humans and can be used as a weapon — the ball can attach to a face and turn a person into jelly

The Beast controls the Ood and uses them to help him try to escape.

QUEEN VICTORIA STARTED
THE TORCHWOOD INSTITUTE
IN 1879, IN ORDER TO INVESTIGATE
AND FIGHT ALIEN HAPPENINGS ON EARTH.
THE INSTITUTE WAS NAMED IN HONOUR OF SIR
ROBERT MACLEISH'S HOME, WHERE SIR ROBERT GAVE
HIS LIFE IN ORDER TO DEFEND HIS QUEEN FROM
AN ALIEN WEREWOLF. THROUGHOUT THEIR
TRAVELS, THE DOCTOR AND ROSE COME
ACROSS THE TORCHWOOD INSTITUTE
TIME AND TIME AGAIN...

During the Sycorax Invasion, Prime Minister Harriet Jones called upon Torchwood to destroy the retreating Sycorax spaceship, as a message to other alien races that the earth is defended. Torchwood used weapons they developed from technology found on a Jathaa Sun Glider, ten years earlier. Their motto became "if it's alien, it's ours", and they collected and learned all they could from other worlds.

At the Tyler's party on the Parallel earth, Pete asked his friend Steve how things were going at Torchwood... While back on our earth, LINDA were using stolen Torchwood files to try and track down the Doctor.

Rose and the Doctor ran into Torchwood again back in the 1950s, while investigating the mysterious Wire. And when they found themselves on Sanctuary Base Six, a space station strangely circling a black hole, Captain Zachary Cross Flane was there to represent the Torchwood Archive.

Whenever they find themselves on Earth, or with humans in any time or part of space, the Torchwood Institute seems to haunt the Doctor and Rose. But as investigators of alien activity, are they friend or foe to the Doctor?

TORCHWOOD IS AN ANAGRAM FOR SOMETHING... MIX THE LETTERS AROUND AND SEE WHAT YOU CAN COME UP WITH!

Answer: Torchwood is an anagram of Doctor Who!

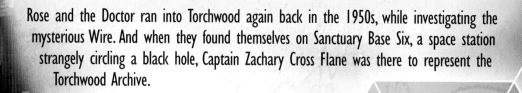

YOU COULD GIVE YOUR NEXT BIRTHDAY PARTY A DOCTOR WHO THEME — BUT WHY WAIT UNTIL YOUR BIRTHDAY? YOU CAN THROW A PARTY OR HOLD A SLEEPOVER IN HONOUR OF YOUR FAVOURITE TIME LORD AT ANY TIME — AND HERE'S HOW!

Rose couldn't resist stepping inside the TARDIS and taking off on an adventure with the Doctor — and your mates will want to come to your party if you make these TARDIS invitations!

FOLD A SHEET OF BLUE PAPER IN HALF. OPEN OUT THE PAPER AND FOLD THE EDGES INTO THE FOLD IN THE MIDDLE. DECORATE THE OUTER FLAPS TO LOOK LIKE THE OUTSIDE OF THE TARDIS USING A BLACK FELT-TIP AND SOME SQUARES OF WHITE PAPER.

WRITE THE DETAILS OF YOUR PARTY INSIDE THE TARDIS — YOU COULD STICK A PICTURE OF THE DOCTOR IN THERE AS WELL!

LOOK AT THE INSIDE OF THE TARDIS. IT'S PRETTY BONKERS, BUT IT'S ALSO KIND OF COOL! WHY NOT DECORATE YOUR PARTY SPACE TO LOOK LIKE THE INSIDE OF SOME SORT OF TIME TRAVELLING MACHINE?

Plastic-coated washing line cord makes good trailing wires, and you could stick foil pie dishes to the wall to make TARDIS-like 'roundels'.

The centrepiece of your room should be a control hub. It shouldn't look slick like modern-day gadgets — more like an organic fusion of past and future technology, just like the TARDIS! Make it as big as you can using old cardboard boxes. Paint them black or cover them with dark paper and bits of foil. If you've got an old and broken cassette player, word processor or something like that, ask a grown-up if he or she can take it apart, so you can use bits, like old circuit boards and push buttons, to stick onto your hub.

Draw around your hand and make a security panel for the door. Everyone who enters the room must put their hand on the panel and have their palm print ID recognized!

KEEP THE LIGHT LEVELS IN THE ROOM REALLY LOW SO EVERYTHING LOOKS A BIT MYSTERIOUS!

TIME FLIES WHEN YOU'RE HAVING FUN — OR TRAVELLING IN THE TARDIS! UNLESS YOU'RE A FRIEND OF THE DOCTOR, YOU WON'T BE TRAVELLING IN THE TARDIS ANY TIME SOON — BUT YOU CAN HAVE FUN PLAYING THESE GAMES AT YOUR DOCTOR WHO PARTY OR SLEEPOVER!

PEOPLE OF THE FUTURE

Who could imagine that the last surviving human would be little more than a flap of skin with a brain in a jar? Get a stack of old magazines and catalogues. Give everyone a piece of paper, pair of scissors, a felt-tip pen and a glue stick. Then cut out different heads and body parts and create new kinds of human life forms. Give your people of the future as many arms and legs, or eyes and mouths as you want. Or giant hands! Or a miniature head! It's up to you! See who can make the funniest human, or the scariest…

If you know someone with lots of old car magazines, see if you can use them to create a new kind of vehicle to handle the terrain on a planet nobody even knows about yet!

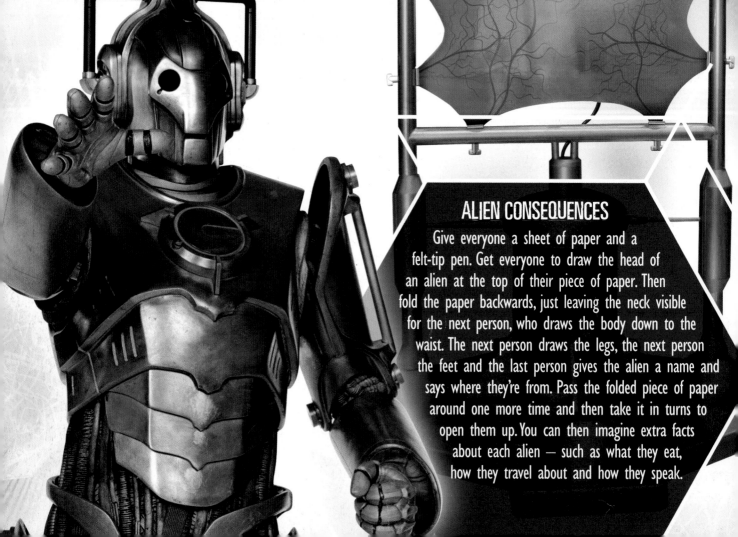

ALIEN CONSEQUENCES

Give everyone a sheet of paper and a felt-tip pen. Get everyone to draw the head of an alien at the top of their piece of paper. Then fold the paper backwards, just leaving the neck visible for the next person, who draws the body down to the waist. The next person draws the legs, the next person the feet and the last person gives the alien a name and says where they're from. Pass the folded piece of paper around one more time and then take it in turns to open them up. You can then imagine extra facts about each alien — such as what they eat, how they travel about and how they speak.

DARK DRAWINGS

Get everyone sitting down with a piece of paper and a pen. Switch off the lights and ask them to draw the TARDIS. Wait until everyone's finished and then get them to draw the Doctor, by the side of the TARDIS. Again, wait until they've finished and then ask them to draw a Dalek attacking the Doctor. And then ask them to draw Rose and so on! Keep going until everyone's had enough and then switch on the lights and see what everyone's drawn! The results are often crazy, no matter how hard you try!

When you're done, you could try making up a spooky story and get everyone to illustrate it (in the dark again, of course!) and see what they come up with!

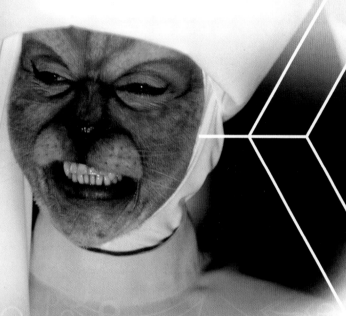

DOCTOR WORDS

Think of a character, or characters, from Doctor Who — such as The Emperor Dalek or The Sisters of Plenitude. Write the name at the top of a sheet of paper. Then set a time limit, say, ten minutes, to make up as many words as you can from the letters of the character's name. Score by giving a point for each word of three or more letters.

ALIEN DRESS UP

See who can put together the freakiest alien look by combining clothes from a dressing-up box. If you have a digital camera, take instant pictures so everyone can see how hilarious they look!

If you don't have a dressing-up box, then get everyone into teams of two and give each team a bunch of props (e.g. a newspaper, old magazines, safety scissors, marker pens, sticky tape) and see who can make the weirdest alien costume in ten minutes.

MYSTERY BOXES

Fill ten little boxes, with ten different dry materials. Seal each box with tape and label them 1 to 10. Ask everyone to make a list and see if they can guess what's inside each box — without using a sonic screwdriver! Try shaking, or even smelling the boxes. At the end of the game, open them all up and see who has got the most correct answers. Try using: rice grains, paperclips, granulated sugar, a pebble, a cotton wool ball, popcorn, peanuts and so on.

⬡ WEREWOLF ATTACK!

WEREWOLVES ARE ATTACKING, AND SOMEONE MUST INSERT THE KOH-I-NOOR DIAMOND IN THE TELESCOPE TO DEFEAT THEM. BUT THE TELESCOPE IS IN THE OBSERVATORY AT THE VERY TOP OF TORCHWOOD HOUSE. CAN YOU EVADE THE WOLVES AND MAKE IT TO THE TOP?

YOU WILL NEED:
• 2-4 PLAYING PIECES
• A DIE

Photocopy or trace the playing pieces and stick them on to cardboard. Alternatively you can use buttons or counters.

Roll a die to see who starts. The person who rolls the highest number goes first. (If two people both get the same highest number, they should roll again.)

Players take it in turns to roll the die, and move their playing pieces forward by the number of squares shown on the die. If the player reaches the bottom of a mistletoe bough, he or she can climb it to the square at the top. However, if the player reaches the top of a wolf's tail, he or she must slide down to the square at the tail's tip.

The first person to reach the final square is the winner.

100 FINISH	99	98
81	82	83
80	79	78
61	62	63
60	59	58
41	42	43
40	39	38
21	22	23
20	19	18
1 START	2	3

97	96	95	94	93	92	91
84	85	86	87	88	89	90
77	76	75	74	73	72	71
64	65	66	67	68	69	70
57	56	55	54	53	52	51
44	45	46	47	48	49	50
37	36	35	34	33	32	31
24	25	26	27	28	29	30
17	16	15	14	13	12	11
4	5	6	7	8	9	10

WHICH ALIEN ARE YOU MOST LIKE?

SOME OF THE ALIENS THE DOCTOR MEETS ON HIS TRAVELS ACROSS THE UNIVERSE ARE ALL TOO HUMAN IN THEIR WEAKNESSES AND PECULIARITIES. SO, DO YOU HAVE MORE IN COMMON WITH THE FEARSOME DALEKS OR THE FRIENDLY FACE OF BOE? FIND OUT WITH THIS QUIZ!

1. IF YOU COULD TRAVEL ANYWHERE IN SPACE AND TIME, WHERE WOULD YOU GO?
A. Forward in time, to see the end of the Earth.
B. Back in time, to see the beginning of the Earth.
C. Forward, to a time when you will the rule the galaxy.
D. Back, to a time when you were young and beautiful.

2. WHAT KIND OF CAR WOULD YOU MOST LIKE TO DRIVE?
A. Something extremely powerful, but not necessarily flashy.
B. Cars are bad for the environment — besides, you can close your eyes and travel in your mind.
C. Who needs a car when you can fly?
D. A classic automobile, updated with the latest gadgets.

3. IF YOU HAD THE OPPORTUNITY, WHAT WOULD YOU CHANGE ABOUT YOURSELF?
A. Get a bigger weapon.
B. You'd like to open up your consciousness to be even more receptive to the wisdom of others.
C. You are perfect — it's everyone else who needs to change.
D. Get rid of those wrinkles around your eyes.

4. HOW WOULD YOU DESCRIBE YOUR IDEAL HOLIDAY?
A. Something adventurous, involving conquering a few small planets.
B. A trip to an exotic place, to see the way other people live.
C. You can never take a holiday from the important job of being you.
D. Being pampered in a luxury health spa.

5. YOU'VE JUST WITNESSED THE END OF THE WORLD AS WE KNOW IT. HOW DO YOU FEEL?
A. Like rejoicing.
B. Sad, for all the things you'll never see again.
C. What do you mean, "How do I feel"? What are feelings?
D. Like eating chips.

MOSTLY AS.
Just like a Cyberman, you're always questing for more power. No matter how many of the latest gadgets you use to soup up your bedroom, house or car there's something slightly old-fashioned about your ambition to be bigger, stronger and faster than everybody else. Try to be happy for other people and you'll be happier in yourself.

MOSTLY BS.
Wise and benevolent, you're most like The Face of Boe. You certainly know other people, you can almost get inside their minds — but do you really know yourself? Perhaps it's time you broke out of that serious

MOSTLY CS.
You are as single-minded and ruthless as a Dalek. It is true that you command respect wherever you go, but then, you have surrounded yourself with like-minded people who never challenge your point of view. Try to get out more, without blowing anything up.

MOSTLY DS.
Quick-witted and with a bad attitude, you're most like Cassandra. OK, she's not an alien but the last living human doesn't look like anyone you know now! Just like Cassandra, you care about your appearance and appreciate the finer things in life but remember:

ANSWER THE QUESTIONS TO FILL IN THE SPIRAL, USING THE LAST LETTER OF EACH WORD AS THE FIRST LETTER OF THE NEXT.

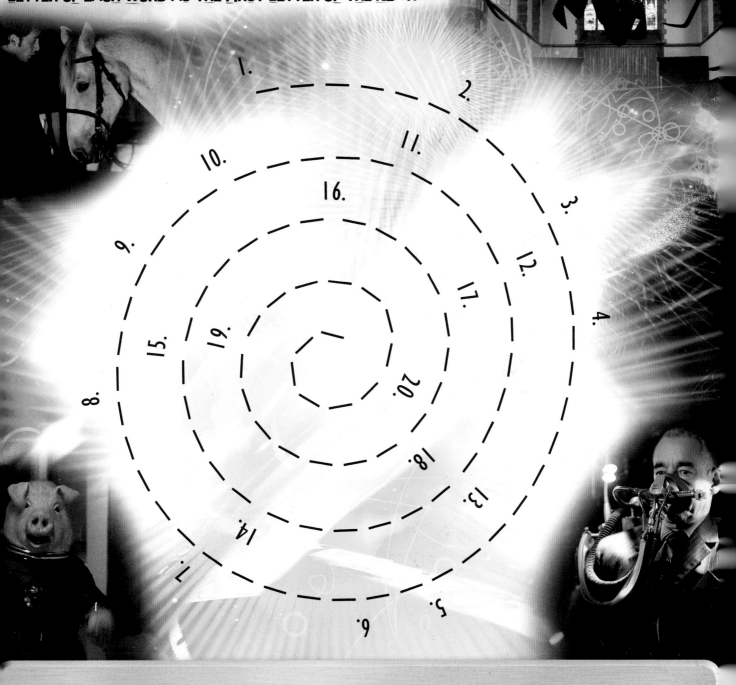

1. Welsh city where the Doctor met Charles Dickens (7)
2. Servant at Torchwood House (5)
3. Companion whom the Doctor soon abandoned (4)
4. Head of the Sisterhood on New Earth (6, 4)
5. Animal modified by the Slitheen to act as a decoy (3)
6. Pete Tyler's call sign on the Parallel Earth (6)
7. Wife of Sir Robert MacLeish (6)
8. Creator of the parallel Earth Cybermen (5)
9. Cassandra's clone servant (4)
10. First word on the sign above the TARDIS door (6)

11. Rose's home planet (5)
12. Department store where Rose once worked (7)
13. Fruit used by the Doctor to defeat the Sycorax leader (7)
14. Horse adopted by the Doctor (6)
15. Creatures attracted to wounds in time (7)
16. Owner of a Welsh funeral parlour (5)
17. Creature found in Van Statten's museum (5)
18. Diamond used to defeat the werewolves (3-1-4)
19. Ricky's grandmother (4-4)
20. Agent of the Mighty Jagrafess (6)

SLITHEEN

THE SLITHEEN ARE A CRIMINAL FAMILY FROM THE PLANET RAXACORICOFALLAPATORIOUS. EXILED FROM THEIR HOME PLANET, THEY FACE THE DEATH PENALTY IF THEY RETURN.

Body made from living calcium

Ability to smell human fear helps them to hunt

Compression field gadget shrinks them to fit into human skins. This compression causes the gas that makes them burp and fart

Excess poison can be exhaled through the lungs

Huge claws for hunting

Females can manufacture poison darts within their fingers

The power of the TARDIS caused Blon Fel Fotch to regress to childhood, enabling her to begin life again.

Zip in forehead of human skins.

HELP BLON FEL FOTCH ESCAPE FROM RAXACORICOFALLAPATORIUS. ONE PATH LEADS TO HER TRIBOPHYSICAL WAVEFORD MACRO-KINETIC EXTRAPOLATOR AND FREEDOM – BUT THE OTHERS WILL PUT HER IN DEADLY DANGER...

START

THE DOCTOR

HUNTERS

FINISH

AS THE DOCTOR WELL KNOWS, SOMETIMES THINGS THAT SEEM LIKE MAGIC CAN BE EXPLAINED AWAY WITH LOGIC OR SCIENCE. TRY THESE EXPERIMENTS ON YOUR OWN AND THEN REPEAT THEM IN FRONT OF FRIENDS AND THEY'LL THINK YOU CAN DO MAGIC!

BLACK HOLE

Reckon you can pass your whole body through a hole in a sheet of A4 paper? It doesn't seem possible, does it? But the trick is to make a really big hole by folding and cutting the paper...

1. Fold your sheet of paper in half. Make a cut on the folded side, close to the edge of the paper. Don't cut all the way across.

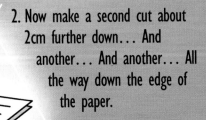

2. Now make a second cut about 2cm further down... And another... And another... All the way down the edge of the paper.

3. Turn the paper around and do the same thing from the other side, cutting in between each of the cuts on the other side of the paper.

4. Now, cut along the folded edge of the central part of paper, leaving the two ends intact.

5. Stretch out the paper and step through the hole!

STRANGE STRIP

A piece of paper has two sides right? Well, try this. Cut a strip off the long side of a sheet of A4 paper. Make a single twist in it and tape the two ends together. Now take a felt-tip pen and draw a line on one side of the strip. What happens...? It's only got one side!

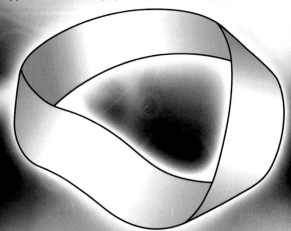

You've just made something called a Möbius Strip, named after August Ferdinand Möbius, a nineteenth century German mathematician and astronomer.

Now try cutting all the way along the line you've just drawn. What do you think will happen?

CLIP TRICK

While you're making strips of paper, try this trick on a mate. Bet him or her that you can link together two paper clips without touching them. Fold a strip of paper, about 12cm long, in half and use the first paper clip to clip the two halves together, about 2cm from the ends. Fold the strip in half again, over the paper clip. Use the second paper clip to clip the paper together as shown below. Pull the two ends of the strip of paper apart — quick sharp! The two paper clips jump into the air and will be linked together when they land.

GET KNOTTED!

If you're making bets with your mates, you might as well try this trick as well. Challenge your mates to tie a knot in your school tie without letting go of the ends. When they've given up trying, show them how it's done! Lay the tie down on a table. Fold your arms and grab an end of the tie in each hand. When you uncross your arms, a knot will appear in the middle of the tie!

MIND BENDER

Try this, it's amazing! Hold a piece of paper against your forehead and write your name on it. Take the piece of paper away from your head and look at it... Have you written your name in backwards mirror writing? It's really hard not to because your brain is thinking about the other side of the paper against your head, and imagining the letters facing that way.

TRICKY QUESTION

Finally, here's a riddle for you... How many people can you get in an empty TARDIS?

The answer? None! As soon as someone steps inside the TARDIS, it's not empty any more!

AH! SO THESE ANDROIDS HAVE DONE YOU OUT OF A JOB - AND HELL HATH NO FURY LIKE A VEXED EX-EMPLOYEE.

COO-EEE!

WHU...

KICK!

GRAB HIS WEAPON!

WHAT'S GOING ON, DOCTOR?

I SHUT OFF THE POWER TO THE MAIN GRID. THE EMERGENCY LIGHTS SHOULD KICK IN ANY SECOND NOW... PLEASE TELL ME YOU GOT THE WEAPON, ROSE.

YEAH - I GOT THE WEAPON.

MINUTES LATER.

WHAT'S GOING TO HAPPEN TO THAT GUY?

OH, HE'LL GO TO PRISON FOR A WHILE -

BUT WHEN HE COMES OUT HE'LL LEAD THE REBELLION AGAINST THE ANDROIDS AND ULTIMATELY SAVE HUMANKIND.

I NEVER KNOW IF YOU ARE SERIOUS, OR JUST MAKING UP STORIES.

AND ANYWAY, YOU MISQUOTED SHAKESPEARE. EVEN I KNOW IT'S "HELL HATH NO FURY LIKE A WOMAN SCORNED".

YEAH? YOU FORGET I'VE BEEN AROUND A LONG TIME!

WHAT, ARE YOU SAYING SHAKESPEARE WAS MISQUOTING YOU WHEN HE WROTE THAT?

OH, I'M NO GOOD AT MAKING UP STORIES - I LEAVE THAT UP TO YOU LOT...

THE END.

THE SYCORAX INVASION OF EARTH WAS PROMPTED BY THEIR DISCOVERY OF GUINEVERE ONE, AN UNMANNED SPACE PROBE SENT TO MARS TO CHART THE LANDSCAPE. THE PROBE HAD A PLAQUE ON IT, IDENTIFYING THE HUMAN RACE FOR ANY ALIENS THAT MAY HAVE COME ACROSS IT IN THE FUTURE. IT ALSO CONTAINED VARIOUS HUMAN ARTEFACTS, LIKE MAPS, MUSIC, WATER, AND EVEN A SAMPLE OF A+ HUMAN BLOOD.

YOU WILL NEED:
- A LARGE JAR OR TIN WITH A LID
- PARCEL TAPE • PLASTIC BAG
- MARKER PEN
- OBJECTS FOR TIME CAPSULE

YOU CAN MAKE YOUR OWN TIME CAPSULE, BY FOLLOWING THE INSTRUCTIONS BELOW, THOUGH BE WARNED, IF THE WRONG PERSON (OR CREATURE!) OPENS IT, IT MAY LEAD TO ALIEN INVASION...!

1. Begin by making sure the jar or tin is completely clean and dry on the inside. If it is damp inside, then some of the things you put in the capsule may not last very long!

DECIDE WHAT YOU WANT TO PUT IN YOUR CAPSULE. SOME IDEAS MIGHT BE:
- A RECENT PHOTO OF YOURSELF, OR YOUR FAMILY
- A CD OF YOUR FAVOURITE SONGS
- A NEWSPAPER OR MAGAZINE
- COINS
- SMALL TOYS

DO NOT PUT FOOD, LIQUIDS OR ANYTHING THAT MAY ROT OR SPILL IN YOUR CAPSULE, OR YOU MIGHT RUIN THE OTHER ITEMS

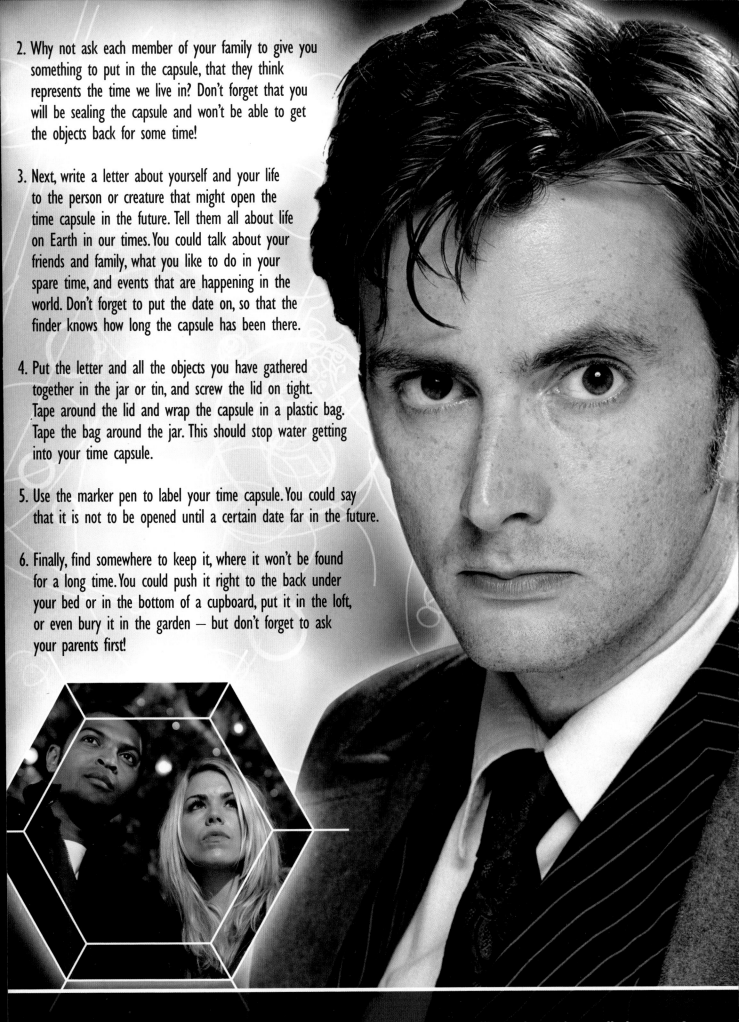

2. Why not ask each member of your family to give you something to put in the capsule, that they think represents the time we live in? Don't forget that you will be sealing the capsule and won't be able to get the objects back for some time!

3. Next, write a letter about yourself and your life to the person or creature that might open the time capsule in the future. Tell them all about life on Earth in our times. You could talk about your friends and family, what you like to do in your spare time, and events that are happening in the world. Don't forget to put the date on, so that the finder knows how long the capsule has been there.

4. Put the letter and all the objects you have gathered together in the jar or tin, and screw the lid on tight. Tape around the lid and wrap the capsule in a plastic bag. Tape the bag around the jar. This should stop water getting into your time capsule.

5. Use the marker pen to label your time capsule. You could say that it is not to be opened until a certain date far in the future.

6. Finally, find somewhere to keep it, where it won't be found for a long time. You could push it right to the back under your bed or in the bottom of a cupboard, put it in the loft, or even bury it in the garden — but don't forget to ask your parents first!

Hopefully, a creature from another planet or someone far in the future will find it and learn all about you! Or, maybe you can open it yourself in a few years time, and look at all the objects from your past!

THE DOCTOR HAS FOUGHT THE DALEKS MANY TIMES, YET EACH TIME HE THINKS HE HAS DEFEATED THEM, THEY FIND A WAY TO RETURN. INSIDE THE METAL CASING IS A MUTATED HUMANOID, WITH ALL EMOTION REMOVED.

DALEK

5ft 6" tall

Lights indicate when Dalek is speaking

Mid-section can be opened to expose creature within

Sucker arm can pick up objects or be used as a weapon

Capable of flying upstairs

Laser gun

After the Time War, the Time Lords trapped all the Daleks in the Genesis Ark, but they eventually found a way to escape...

Four special Daleks were not captured during the Time War. They became the Cult of Skaro, and plotted for the Dalek's revenge.

ROSE HAS WRITTEN A LETTER TO HER MUM – BUT IT'S BEEN INFILTRATED BY TEN DIFFERENT ALIENS AND VILLAINS! ROSE HAS TRACKED DOWN THE FIRST ONE, BUT CAN YOU HELP HER OUT BY FINDING THE OTHERS?

Dear Mum,

How are you? We've been travelling round the universe as usual, visiting planets like Jarsyco, Raxacoricofallapatorius and Tamkamela VI. That was a funny place – it's like Olde England in the days when there were wolves and bears and everyone said 'verily'. Couldn't have coped there long – they didn't even have any muesli, the entire population ate roast boar for breakfast. I didn't fancy that at all, especially as the tribe we were visiting just left the carcass and ran off, leaving me to clear it all up. 'You are a person most helpful, a veritable angel,' the leader said to me afterwards, but I felt more like a vulture.

Then we had to decide where to go next. The subject of Mardi Gras kept coming up, but we finally ended up in America in the 1940s. We made friends with two boys, Neil and Alek, who loved the idea of going into space. The Doctor gave them a pretend space flight – you should have seen him: 'six, seven, seal the hatch – eight, nine, ready engines – ten, eleven, take off!' Neil said he wanted to be the first astronaut on the moon. Well, you never know...

See you soon,

love Rose xxx

DOOMSDAY!

WHEN THE DOCTOR AND ROSE WENT TO VISIT ROSE'S MUM AND SHE INTRODUCED THEM TO A GHOST, THEY HAD NO IDEA THAT THEY WOULD SOON BE INVOLVED IN AN EPIC ADVENTURE INVOLVING A TOP SECRET ORGANIZATION, CYBERMEN AND DALEKS...

Ghosts were appearing all over the world — vague, misty shapes of people, which everyone thought were their dead friends and relatives returned to this world. What they didn't know was that the 'ghosts' were being brought here from another universe.

Torchwood is a top secret organization set up by Queen Victoria after the Doctor and Rose saved her from attack by a werewolf. She decided there should be a secret group that defended the British Empire against other-worldly threats — The Torchwood Institute. But what the scientists and soldiers at Torchwood did not realize was that they were making the threat even greater. They were experimenting on a mysterious sphere that arrived from another dimension. And their experiments were making the ghosts appear.

But as the Doctor and Rose were to find out, the ghosts were not people at all. They were Cybermen, coming through from the world where they had been created to invade our own Earth. An advance guard of Cybermen took over Torchwood, and opened the way for the ghosts to appear fully, as an army of millions of Cybermen.

The armies of the world tried to hold back the Cybermen, but bullets would not stop the huge metal figures. The Cybermen were everywhere. It wasn't an invasion so much as a conquest.

But even the Cybermen didn't know *how* they were able to come through from their world. They didn't know that the strange sphere was actually a Void Ship that had weakened the boundary between the different universes. Inside the Void Ship were the creatures that had been hiding outside time and space, waiting for their own chance to emerge and conquer — Daleks!

The Daleks inside the ship were the Cult of Skaro. A special group of Daleks whose job it was to make sure the Dalek race survived the terrible Time War against the Time Lords, the Doctor's people. They hid in the Void until the war was finished. The Cult of Skaro was led by a black Dalek, and the four Daleks even had names. Their job was to try to think like the enemy so as to find ways to defeat them. They were called Thay, Sec, Rabe and Caan. It was all part of becoming enough like the enemy to predict and counter their actions.

The Doctor and Rose had been joined by Mickey and Rose's father, who came through from the other world to fight the Cybermen. As the Doctor, Rose and Mickey worked to try to find a way to save the world, the Daleks and Cybermen fought a terrible battle. The Cybermen were determined not to let the Daleks stop them invading and conquering Earth. The Daleks saw the Cybermen as inferior beings to be defeated and destroyed. They knew that one Dalek could destroy thousands of Cybermen, but on Earth there were now millions of Cybermen out to destroy just four Daleks.

The Daleks had a secret. They had brought with them a large casket they called the Genesis Ark. They had stolen it from the Time Lords themselves; something that they knew would guarantee the survival of the Dalek race. It was a Time Lord prison. Inside were all the Daleks the Time Lords had captured over the course of the long Time War, waiting to be released.

The Daleks opened the Genesis Ark and an army of Daleks poured out to attack the Cybermen. The Cybermen's weapons had no effect on the Daleks, and it looked as if the Daleks would easily defeat the Cybermen. But the Doctor and his friends had other ideas. Jackie went back with them through the Void as the Doctor and Rose struggled to close the opening through to the other world. They managed it — hurling the Daleks and Cybermen into the Void between worlds and trapping them there.

The Doctor had won, but at a cost. Mickey and Rose's parents were now back in the other world, with no way for the Doctor ever to see them again. And as the opening closed, Rose too was pulled through. Will the Doctor and Rose ever see each other again...?

THE TARDIS HAS TAKEN THE DOCTOR TO MEET ALL SORTS OF PEOPLE (NOT TO MENTION HORSES). SEE HOW MANY OF THEIR NAMES YOU CAN FIND IN THE GRID. NAMES MAY BE HIDDEN UP, DOWN, BACKWARDS, FORWARDS OR DIAGONALLY.

O	T	E	N	N	A	A	T	I	R	I	S
S	I	R	R	O	B	E	R	T	I	N	T
A	N	G	E	L	O	D	I	J	T	T	R
I	A	D	G	S	P	D	N	S	A	R	O
N	S	R	I	A	R	I	E	J	N	T	L
D	Q	A	T	A	M	R	R	A	N	L	A
R	U	H	T	R	A	E	I	N	E	T	F
A	I	T	A	F	T	L	D	H	D	T	F
G	T	I	F	S	B	Y	C	R	R	A	A
A	H	M	I	U	Q	T	A	E	O	R	R
N	R	S	U	K	I	E	E	I	I	D	L
E	L	E	B	M	R	S	D	N	D	I	O
S	A	N	M	I	S	O	B	E	L	S	N
H	T	A	P	D	E	R	D	T	E	A	Y
T	D	J	S	E	O	R	S	R	N	R	E
A	G	H	I	E	T	T	E	N	I	E	R
R	A	A	D	N	Q	U	I	C	R	C	O
D	M	R	R	S	N	E	K	C	I	D	K
I	E	A	A	R	E	Y	N	O	L	D	S
S	D	S	T	R	I	C	K	L	A	N	D

ADAM MITCH[ELL]
ANGELO
ANNE-DROID
ARTHUR
ASQUITH
DE MAGGIO
DICKENS
INDRA GANES[H]
ISOBEL
RAFFALO
REDPATH
REINETTE
REYNOLDS
RICKY
RITA-ANNE
RODRICK
ROSE TYLER
SARAH JANE S[MITH]
SIR ROBERT
SISTER JATT
SNEED
STRICKLAND
SUKI
TREES
TRIN-E

LIKE THE DALEKS, THE CYBERMEN ARE ONE OF THE DOCTOR'S OLDEST ENEMIES AND HE HAS COME ACROSS THEM MANY TIMES. ALTHOUGH THEY LOOK LIKE ROBOTS, THEY WERE ACTUALLY ONCE HUMAN, BUT HAVE HAD ALL THEIR LIMBS AND ORGANS REPLACED WITH ARTIFICIAL ONES.

CYBERMEN

Electronically generated voice

Over 6ft 7"

Inbuilt energy blaster

Metal armour

Plastic and steel replace flesh and bone

The Cybermen were built in a Cybus Industries factory on a parallel earth.

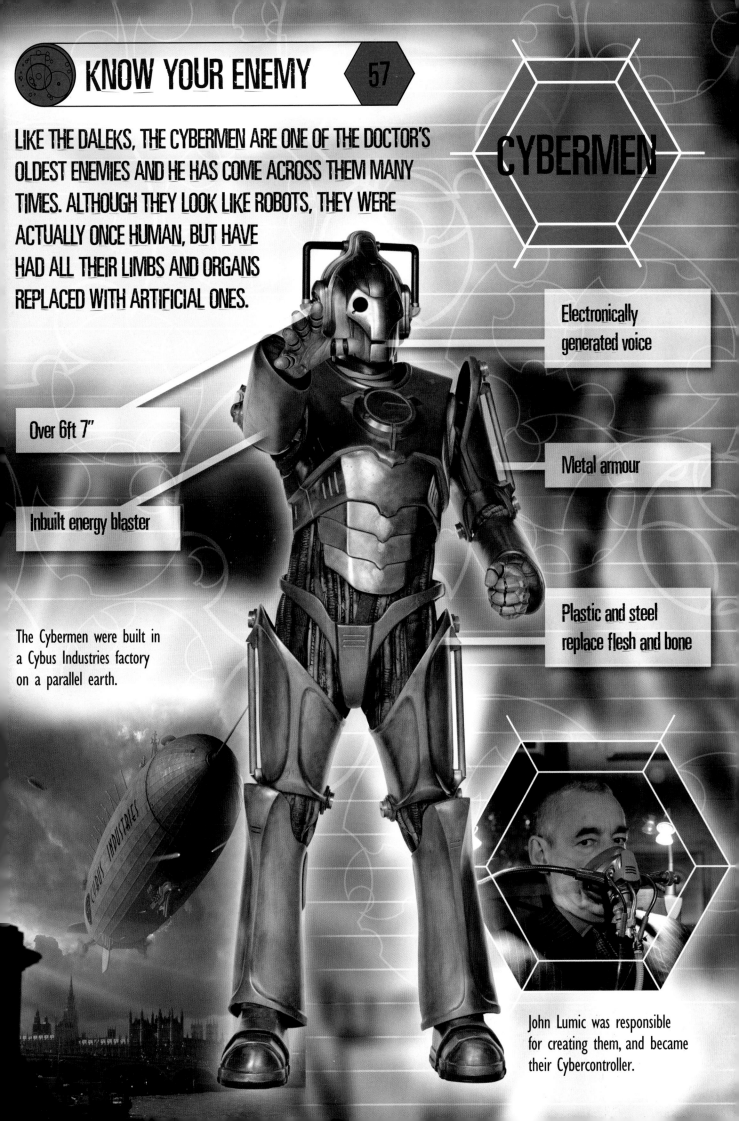

John Lumic was responsible for creating them, and became their Cybercontroller.

ACT LIKE A TIME LORD!

AS YOU KNOW BY NOW, FROM TIME TO TIME IT IS
IMPORTANT FOR THE DOCTOR TO REGENERATE. EACH
TIME HE DOES, HIS APPEARANCE COMPLETELY CHANGES.
AND HE HAS HAD SOME PRETTY WACKY OUTFITS IN THE
PAST! HERE'S HOW YOU CAN CONVINCE EVERYONE AROUND
YOU THAT YOU'RE A TIME LORD!

Wear an eccentric item of clothing – all year round and whatever the weather. You could wear a floppy hat and an impossibly long stripy scarf – even in summer. Or how about a sharp suit, long coat and trainers. Or a frilly shirt and velvet smoking jacket, together with sharply creased trousers, highly polished shoes and a cape. These are the clothes that are sure to gain you respect whether you're walking through Roman Britain or simply recharging your batteries on a distant planet.

Get yourself a companion. The Doctor always has at least one companion, someone he can trust to travel with him to the ends of the Earth… And beyond! You can trick your best mate into being your companion by just not telling them you're a Time Lord. However, he or she might not be as enthusiastic as Rose Tyler when you ask them to accompany you to the planet Raxicoricofallapatorius.

Pretend you've just come back from a distant planet by adopting some of the habits you've seen there. Anyone can come back from Holland with a few words of Dutch, or bring a sombrero back from Spain. But only you can get away with spitting, instead of saying hello, as that is the traditional way of greeting the Moxx of Balhoon.

Time Lords don't like violence and avoid unnecessary confrontation. So try and talk your way out of trouble if you can. You can always use your crazy clothes as a distraction.

Always carry a little bit of special technology with you and never explain how it works. Psychic paper is good, as long as you don't have to use it. Alternatively, pick up any pocket-sized household object and keep it about your person. When people ask you why you've got a spoon in your pocket tell them, "It's a sonic spoon and it's much better for disarming people than any kind of weapon. Plus I can eat soup with it, should the opportunity arise."

Be flippant about time. Hey, you're a Time Lord! So what if you're ten minutes late? Just say you turned up on time when you lived through this day on a previous occasion and nothing interesting happened so you decided to turn up late this time. If nothing else, this usually confuses people enough to stop them arguing with you.

MAKE SURE YOU HAVE A SENSE OF HUMOUR – IF YOU DON'T LAUGH AT YOURSELF, SOMEONE ELSE
WILL ESPECIALLY IN THAT FRILLY SHIRT AND EXCESSIVELY LONG SCARF

Page 15

MONSTER HUNT

		T	O	R	C	H	W	O	O	D
			S	Y	C	O	R	A	X	
K	R	O	N	K	B	U	R	G	E	R
M	I	S	T	L	E	T	O	E		
		J	A	G	R	A	F	E	S	S
G	R	E	E	N	M	O	O	N		
		P	R	E	A	C	H	E	R	S
	H	A	R	K	N	E	S	S		

Page 24

K-9'S CAFÉ CONFUSION

The Doctor ordered ginger beer.
Rose ordered cola.
Mickey ordered coffee.
Sarah Jane ordered tea.
Kenny ordered orange juice.

Page 28-29

SPACIAL AWARENESS

1. Venus is closer to the Earth than Mars.
2. Mercury — because Mercury turns so slowly on its axis, the time it takes for the sun to appear twice directly overhead is longer than the time it takes for the planet to orbit the sun.
3. Jupiter is 11 times wider than Earth, yet a 'day' there lasts 9 hours and 55 minutes!
4. Uranus — it tilts from the vertical at almost 98°C.
5. Mars — the Olympus Mons is three times taller than Everest!
6. Pluto's diameter is 2,274 km; the Earth's Moon has a diameter of 3,476 km.
7. Uranus — Juliet, Cressida and Desdemona are named after characters from the writings of William Shakespeare.
8. Mercury — it can be as hot as 450°C during the day and as cold as -180°C at night.
9. Venus or Uranus — seen from their North poles, all the planets rotate counterclockwise, except for Venus and Uranus!
10. E is false. Pluto is actually the smallest planet in the solar system.

The Moon

11. D - July 20th, 1969 was the date of the first manned lunar landing.
12. B - The Apollo mission.
13. C - Meteorites impacting on the Moon's surface are responsible for most of the craters on the Moon.

14. True! Most of the Moon's mountain chains are named after mountain ranges on Earth.
15. This is a trick question! The moon has been thought responsible for all of these things. It does cause the tides of our seas, and has influenced our calendar months. Superstitions also blame it for creating werewolves and helping witches!

The Earth

16. D - 71% of the Earth's surface is covered by water.
17. A - The Great Wall of China.
18. C - Sir Isaac Newton — he also created calculus, discovered that white light is composed of many colours, and developed the laws of motion still in use today.
19. False, the Earth is slightly flattened at the Poles.
20. Geodesy — geodesic surveys of the Earth's surface are commonly made using radio signals and laser beams from satellites!

SO HOW DID YOU DO?

Less than 5

Hey, this was one tricky quiz so you don't need to feel bad! But if you want to travel with the Doctor, you'd better swot up a bit — you can't bend the rules of space travel without knowing a bit about them first!

Between 6 and 12

Well done! You obviously know your planets from your moons and have all the makings of a Time Lord's travelling companion! But don't stop finding out about space — there's so much of it out there, after all!

13 or more

You are either an astronaut or a cheat — or perhaps you're a Time Lord like the Doctor himself! Either way, make sure you use your knowledge wisely and don't end up a waste of space like those dreaded Daleks!

Page 39

GOING ROUND IN CIRCLES

1. Cardiff	11. Earth
2. Flora	12. Henrik's
3. Adam	13. Satsuma
4. Matron Casp	14. Arthur
5. Pig	15. Reapers
6. Gemini	16. Sneed
7. Isobel	17. Dalek
8. Lumic	18. Koh-I-Noor
9. Chip	19. Rita-Anne
10. Police	20. Editor

Escape from Raxacoricofallapatorious

START

THE DOCTOR

HUNTERS

FINISH

Message Madness

Dear Mum,

How are you? We've been travelling round the universe as usual, visiting planets like Jarexyco, Raxacoricofallapatorius and Tamkamela VI. That was a funny place – it's like Olde England in the days when there were wolves and bears and everyone said 'verily'. Couldn't have coped there long – they didn't even have any muesli, the entire population ate roast boar for breakfast. I didn't fancy that at all, especially as the tribe we were visiting just left the carcass and ran off, leaving me to clear it all up. 'You are a person most helpful, a veritable angel,' the leader said to me afterwards, but I felt more like a vulture.

Then we had to decide where to go next. The subject of Mardi Gras kept coming up, but we finally ended up in America in the 1940s. We made friends with two boys, Neil and Alek, who loved the idea of going into space. The Doctor gave them a pretend space flight – you should have seen him: 'six, seven, seal the hatch – eight, nine, ready engines – ten, eleven, take off!' Neil said he wanted to be the first astronaut on the moon. Well, you never know...

See you soon,

love Rose xxx

TARDIS Tracker

O T E N N A A T I R I S
S I R R O B E R T I N T
A N G E L O D I J T T R
I A D G S P D N S A R O
N S R I A R I E J N T L
D Q A T A M R R A N L A
R U H T R A E I N E T F
A I T A F T L D H D T F
G T I F S B Y C R R A A
A H M I U Q T A E O R R
N R S U K I E E I I D L
E L E B M R S D N D I O
S A N M I S O B E L S N
H T A P D E R D T E A Y
T D J S E O R S R N R E
A G H I E T T E N I E R
R A A D N Q U I C R C O
D M R R S N E K C I D K
I E A A R E Y N O L D S
S D S T R I C K L A N D